RAMIFICATIONS OF MODERN CULTURE

DR. ASHWANI KUMAR

DR. BACHITTER SINGH

First Edition of the book is published in 2024

Published by Kindle Direct Publishing

ISBN of Print Edition: 9798343549256

Imprint: Independently published

To Unpredictable times, encounters and people!

CONTENTS

Preface

In this era of rapid transformation, the profound interplay between societal norms, technological advancements, and cultural shifts has reshaped various aspects of human life, creating both opportunities and challenges. This collection of chapters, authored by Dr. Ashwani Kumar, Bachitter Singh and other co-authors, probe into some of the most pressing issues of contemporary society, exploring the dynamics of fashion, social media, emotion, and modernity from a sociological perspective. The chapters of this book were originally published as articles on PureSociology (https://puresociology.com).

Chapter I: Shadows of Fashion in the Contemporary World

Dr. Ashwani Kumar and Dr. Vikas Bhandari examine the pervasive influence of the fashion industry, which often shapes women's perspectives and behaviors. They argue that fashion acts as a subtle yet powerful tool of social control, establishing ideals of beauty and success that women feel compelled to follow. This chapter critiques the fashion industry's role in perpetuating unrealistic standards and suggests ways for women to reclaim their autonomy and redefine beauty on their own terms.

Chapter II: Pleasure and Objectification of the Body in Modern Society

Dr. Kumar and Dr. Bhandari further explore how modern capitalist societies commodify the human body, turning it into a marketable entity. They discuss the complex relationship between body presentation, societal expectations, and individual agency, highlighting the pressure to conform to idealized body images. This chapter calls for a critical examination of how these dynamics affect personal freedom and societal norms.

Chapter III: Shrinking Anger Spaces in Modern Society

In collaboration with Arvind, Dr. Kumar explores the changing dynamics of anger in contemporary society. They argue that modernity's shrinking spaces for expressing anger have led to emotional disequilibrium, potentially increasing crime rates. This chapter emphasizes the need to create constructive outlets for anger to maintain mental well-being and social harmony.

Chapter IV: The Risk of Emerging Virtual Inequality and Marginalization

Dr. Kumar and Dr. Bachitter Singh address the growing inequalities within the virtual realm. They discuss how the digital divide and the emergence of virtual celebrities contribute to new forms of social stratification and marginalization. This chapter underscores the need for equitable digital spaces and the importance of addressing virtual inequality to prevent societal fragmentation.

Chapter V: Exploring the Dynamics of Friendship

Dr. Kumar probe into the complexities of friendship in modern society. He contrasts the traditional kinship model with the more fluid and adaptable nature of contemporary friendships, discussing the challenges and opportunities that arise from this shift. The chapter advocates for a nuanced understanding of friendship, highlighting the need for clearer roles and expectations to foster genuine connections.

Chapter VI: Is Indian Society Experiencing Marketization in the Name of Modernization?

Dr. Kumar & Dr. Singh critically examined the intersection of modernization and marketization in Indian society. They argues that the push for modernity has been conflated with market expansion, leading to a market-toxicated class and exacerbating economic divides. This chapter calls for a more holistic approach to modernization that goes beyond mere consumption and addresses broader societal goals.

Chapter VII: Social Media Reels and Clothing Consumption: Exploring Trends, Influence, and Sustainability

Mr. Amit Kumar explores how social media, particularly reels, influences clothing consumption among young people. The author discuss the symbolic value of clothing, the impact of conspicuous consumption, and the environmental implications of rising demand for both organic and synthetic materials. This chapter emphasizes the need for sustainable fashion practices and mindful consumption.

This compilation aims to provide a comprehensive understanding of these multifarious issues, encouraging readers to critically reflect on the forces shaping contemporary society. By examining the interplay between fashion, social media, emotion, and modernity, the authors offer valuable insights into the challenges and opportunities of living in a rapidly changing world. We hope this work will inspire further research and dialogue on these critical topics, fostering a more inclusive, equitable, and sustainable future.

Chapter I
Shadows of Fashion in the Contemporary World

Dr. Ashwani Kumar and Dr. Vikas Bhandari

In modern times, fashion has developed into a significant influence that can be seen in the clothing styles that are worn. The fashion industry constantly and unknowingly makes women the source of pleasure for people by dictating trends that are constantly shifting and changing. This control is exercised over women's conduct as well as their appearance. The dominance of fashion in today's society, which can be understood as an instrument of colonisation because it moulds women's perspectives and restricts their potential, has cast a shadow over traditional practises and standards.

Furthermore, it is essential to keep in mind that the contemporary institution of fashion is primarily representing the interests of the market rather than expressing the ideals and requirements of society. For instance, the clothing brand Fashion to Figure is known for its commitment to providing inclusive and trendy fashion for women sizes. They offer a variety of clothing options, including dresses, tops, bottoms, outerwear, and accessories, one of their notable aspects is their attention to current fashion trends, ensuring that plus-size women have access to the latest styles and designs. Similarly, Fashion Nova is a popular fashion brand known for its trendy and affordable clothing, primarily targeting a middle-class women. These brand's emphasis on diversity and representation in their marketing and product offerings has contributed to its popularity among customers seeking fashionable options in extended sizes. Within the framework of Indian culture, conventional standards have historically been responsible for imposing stringent limitations on women, relegating them to secondary roles, and limiting their degree of autonomy. On the other hand, as a result of the process of modernization, women have started to contest these conventions and assert themselves in society. Sadly, rather than obtaining complete liberty, women have been confronted with a new type of dominance in the form of the establishment of fashion.

By establishing and popularizing fads to which women are socially pressured to adhere, the fashion industry serves as a sort of social control. The influential members of society who have the power to shape cultural preferences frequently impose these tendencies. As a direct result of this, women are inundated with pictures and messages that define beauty and fashion, which can lead to feelings of inadequacy if they do not fit these ideals. This pressure is the result of the power dynamics at play within the fashion business, where the ruling class and powerful personalities hold the authority to develop and transmit fashion trends. As a result of these power dynamics, the fashion industry is subject to this pressure. It serves their interests to maintain power over society by generating false awareness among women and sustaining the assumption that conforming to fashion trends is vital for acceptance and success. This is accomplished through the use of fashion as a tool to achieve this goal.

Diverting attention away from structural disparities places additional constraints on the agency and freedom of women. In light of this, it is absolutely essential for women in the fashion business to become aware of the power dynamics there and to actively challenge them. They will be able to restore their independence and liberate themselves from the colonializing effect of fashion if they take this step. It is crucial for women to re-imagine what it means to be beautiful and to express themselves in their own unique way, rather than succumbing to the standards that are set by the elite. Women can recover their autonomy and achieve true liberation from the repressive forces of fashion if they take responsibility for their own lives and make a point of expressing their unique identities.

We are able to have a clearer understanding of the repressive nature of this phenomenon if we draw parallels between the institution of fashion and Marx's notion of religion. Along the same lines as religion, fashion may become a tool that is used to impose influence over individuals, thereby molding both their beliefs and their conduct. Fashion acts as a tool that creates a false consciousness. It is essential to provide women with the agency to break away from the standards that are imposed on them and to assert their individuality in order to fight this oppressive influence. They will be able to restore their sovereignty and achieve true independence if they take this step. This procedure entails acknowledging and contesting the prevalent narratives that are perpetuated by the fashion industry, as well as redefining beauty and self-expression according to their own terms. Women have the capacity to demolish oppressive hierarchies and develop a fashion culture that is more empowering and inclusive if they embrace diversity and promote inclusive portrayals. It is impossible to disregard the significance of fashion's role in moulding and influencing the discourse of women in modern society.

Understanding the repressive nature of this phenomenon is possible once we recognize the links between fashion and the Marxian idea of religion. Fashion is a kind of social control. It is vital for women to be given the power to break away from enforced conventions and assert their individuality in order to reclaim their autonomy and accomplish genuine liberty. Women are able to liberate themselves from the colonializing impact of fashion and reach their full potential if they challenge the power dynamics that exist within the fashion industry, as well as redefine beauty and self-expression according to their own standards. The contemporary fashion institution has given birth to fast fashion, encouraged by the modern fashion industry's push for rapid production of affordable clothing, particularly appealing to women. This trend raises the concern that individuals, especially women, may develop consumer cognition, consequently, they may be alienated from political cognition, an essential cognition to survive in a complex political world.

References:

1. Marx, K. (1867). Capital: A critique of political economy*. Progress Publishers.

2. Veblen, T. (1899). The theory of the leisure class: An economic study of institutions. Macmillan.

3. Lipovetsky, G. (1994). The empire of fashion: Dressing modern democracy. Princeton University Press.

4. 4. McRobbie, A. (2009). The aftermath of feminism: Gender, culture and social change. SAGE Publications.

5. Entwistle, J. (2000). The fashioned body: Fashion, dress and modern social theory. Polity Press.

6. Wilson, E. (1985). Adorned in dreams: Fashion and modernity. I.B. Tauris.

7. Eicher, J., & Evenson, S. L. (Eds.). (2000). The visible self: Global perspectives on dress, culture, and society. Fairchild Publications.

8. Fletcher, K., & Grose, L. (2012). Fashion & sustainability: Design for change. Laurence King Publishing.

9. Thomas, D. (2019). Fashionopolis: The price of fast fashion and the future of clothes. Penguin Press.

Chapter II
Pleasure and Objectification of Body in Modern Society

Dr. Ashwani Kumar and Dr. Vikas Bhandari

In the era of modern society, showcasing the body or 'body presentation' has become a popular trend influenced by cultural, social, and economic shifts. Body presentation refers to the ways in which individuals present and display their bodies in various social and cultural contexts. It encompasses not only physical appearance but also gestures, clothing choices, and other nonverbal cues that communicate messages about identity, status, and cultural meanings associated with the body. It often leads to the commodification or objectification of body, a reduction of the body to a marketable or consumable entity, emphasizing the commercial or superficial aspects of showcasing the body.

Foucault argued that there are 'docile bodies' that have been trained, disciplined, and regulated by various institutions and power structures. These bodies are subjected to control and normalization, shaping them to conform to societal standards and expectations. This article explores how the presentation or showcasing of the body having relationship with pleasure in modern capitalist and post-capitalist societies.

Modern platforms frequently depict the freedom to showcase one's body in public. It is a complex landscape in which judgments of attractiveness are not apportioned arbitrarily but rather possess a systematic that both reflects and molds the preferences and attitudes of niche audiences. The institution of modern fashion always tries to set a belief that women's ability to showcase their bodies gives them confidence and a sense of prestige.

In the pervasive culture of body presentation, the commodification of the human form extends its reach into the fabric of everyday life. Advertising, popular media, and social platforms relentlessly contribute to the construction of an idealized body image, fostering unrealistic standards that individuals may feel compelled to emulate. This phenomenon, often fueled by consumerism, perpetuates a cycle where bodies are not only showcased but also meticulously sculpted to fit predefined molds. The pressure to conform to these standards is palpable, creating a nuanced interplay between personal agency and societal expectations. In the pursuit of an idealized presentation, individuals navigate the complexities of self-expression and conformity, negotiating the delicate balance between autonomy and external influences.

The contemporary platforms act as canvases for the liberation of body presentation, portraying it as an empowering act that transcends traditional boundaries. The depiction of individuals showcasing their bodies in public is not merely a spontaneous occurrence; rather, it unfolds within a meticulously crafted landscape where judgments of attractiveness carry a nuanced system. Social media platforms, in particular, perpetuate ideals of beauty that not only reflect but also actively shape the preferences and attitudes of diverse niche audiences. These platforms serve as dynamic arenas where individuals navigate the delicate balance between self-expression and the ever-evolving standards of attractiveness.

Moreover, the institution of modern fashion plays a pivotal role in this narrative, relentlessly promoting the belief that a woman's ability to confidently showcase her body is synonymous with empowerment and prestige. The fashion industry, with its ever-changing trends and ideals, becomes both a mirror and a sculptor of societal values. Women are often bombarded with messages reinforcing the idea that conforming to modern pressures of body presentation is not only a means of self-expression but also a pathway to societal validation. This perpetuates a cycle where the desire for confidence and prestige is intertwined with the external expectations set by the fashion world and the broader social milieu.

However, it is intriguing to know whether people especially women derive pleasure from the showcasing of their bodies in public or whether they have been commodified by market forces and become the source of pleasure for the masses.

The current trend is unmistakably propelled by market forces seeking to commodify bodies and provide pleasure aspirations to a wide array of potential consumers and their workforce. Historically, traditional organizations and customs held considerable sway over notions of the ideal body, dictating specific criteria for women's body presentation that no longer align with the expectations of the contemporary market. These age-old standards, deeply ingrained in societal expectations and often reinforced through various cultural channels, imposed rigid roles and aesthetic norms on women. Nevertheless, with the unfolding of modernity, unprecedented shifts began to emerge. The evolving landscape started challenging these entrenched norms, prompting a reevaluation of societal expectations and fostering a transformation in the way bodies are perceived and presented.

This liberation, however, comes with a twofold impact. On one hand, it has allowed women to break away from traditional constraints, encouraging autonomy in self-expression and choices related to their bodies and intimate lives. On the other hand, it has led to the commodification of women's bodies, positioning them as objects of pleasure in the lens of the masses.

The modern construction of ideal bodies, fueled by media, advertising, and societal norms, has often centered around a particular image of women, emphasizing certain physical attributes and conforming to ever-evolving standards of beauty. Media is always guided by popular trends with the help of the institution of fashion, for instance, institution of fashion created the differentiation of various types of attires. The fashion industry developed the idea for occasion-based attires or dresses like cocktail dresses, a dress code that is suitable for semi-formal events, falling between casual wear and formal wear. It is often requested for events like cocktail parties, weddings, upscale dinners, or other social gatherings that are not strictly black-tie affairs. The goal is to look polished and stylish without being overly formal. If we search cocktail attire for women on Google, we will find the kind of attire that supports the idea of showcasing the body. Similarly, the idea of sexy dresses is also another example that perpetuates the same idea. This commodification and objectification, while granting a degree of freedom, have also imposed new societal expectations, leading to the policing of women's bodies and perpetuating unrealistic beauty standards. Let's consider the case of a dance club where people engage in recreational activities such as dancing and people are free to consume alcoholic drinks. Essentially, we can say that dance clubs as a platform in modern society for seeking pleasure. There is a norm for women to come in cocktail or sexy dresses, commonly known as club dresses. This reflects the idea that the club is also attempting to portray women as a source of pleasure.

In this shift, traditional norms that once compelled women to fit within narrow confines of acceptability have transitioned into a modern framework where women's bodies, though seemingly liberated, are often objectified, and commodified for mass acceptance. Understanding the complexities of modernity's impact on the construction of ideal bodies requires a nuanced perspective one that acknowledges the liberation from traditional constraints while also recognizing the commodification and objectification that modern societal constructs impose. It calls for a continuous dialogue that empowers women to reclaim agency over their bodies and desires, transcending the confines of societal expectations and strengthening a culture of genuine acceptance and autonomy. The question that arises here is: Can the source of pleasure lead a pleasurable life?

References:

1. Foucault, M. (1975). Discipline and punish: The birth of the prison. Random House.

2. Entwistle, J. (2000). The fashioned body: Fashion, dress and modern social theory. Polity Press.

3. McRobbie, A. (2009). The aftermath of feminism: Gender, culture and social change. SAGE Publications.

4. Veblen, T. (1899). The theory of the leisure class: An economic study of institutions. Macmillan.

5. Lipovetsky, G. (1994). The empire of fashion: Dressing modern democracy. Princeton University Press.

6. Fletcher, K., & Grose, L. (2012). Fashion & sustainability: Design for change*. Laurence King Publishing.

7. Thomas, D. (2019). Fashionopolis: The price of fast fashion and the future of clothes. Penguin Press.

8. Wilson, E. (1985). Adorned in dreams: Fashion and modernity*. I.B. Tauris.

Chapter III
Shrinking Anger Spaces in Modern Society

Dr. Ashwani Kumar and Arvind

An Emotion is an Energy in Motion and all energies search vent, laws although not prescribe for an accepted or lawful vent, they (laws) do prescribe for the unaccepted vents and it is these unaccepted vents that are termed as – "CRIME".

In the context of contemporary society, anger is an inherent and universal aspect of human emotions, exerting a substantial impact on mental well-being depending on how it is expressed and managed. The dynamics of anger within modern societies are molded by a complex interplay of factors, including cultural norms, social expectations, and individual coping mechanisms. These elements collectively influence the diverse ways in which individuals navigate and address their emotional experiences, particularly those related to anger. Understanding and effectively managing these dynamics is crucial for nurturing healthy emotional expression and overall mental health in the modern world.

Certainly, there are instances where individuals face challenges in expressing their anger constructively. In certain situations, societal norms discourage the open expression of anger, leading individuals to internalize these emotions. The repercussions of repressed or unexpressed anger can be substantial, potentially contributing to elevated stress levels and, in some cases, acting as a precursor to conditions like depression. Recognizing and appropriately managing anger is a crucial aspect of maintaining mental well-being, emphasizing the importance of addressing this emotion in a healthy and constructive manner.

Medium of Vent in Traditional Societies

"The medium of vent was institutionalized within social boundaries and a hierarchy for vent existed on the same model of Caste system"

Traditional societies were characterized by relatively limited connectivity among larger groups, wherein individuals had distinct opportunities for the management of anger. A case in point is traditional Indian society, where the caste system afforded those in higher castes the liberty to openly express their anger towards individuals in lower castes. This hierarchical structure not only permitted but also institutionalized the venting of anger within defined social boundaries.

Dr. Ashwani Kumarin his article "Sociology of Animals" suggests that individuals with less societal power might have channeled their anger by directing it towards animals. This unconventional yet accepted means of emotional expression highlights the unique ways in which traditional societies provided outlets for individuals with varying power dynamics to manifest their anger.

The social structures and norms inherent in traditional settings often facilitated specific channels for the venting or manifestation of anger, acknowledging the human need for emotional expression within established boundaries. These outlets, although embedded in hierarchical frameworks, served as mechanisms for releasing pent-up emotions and contributed to the overall emotional equilibrium within these societies. Understanding the historical dynamics of anger management in traditional contexts offers insights into the evolving ways in which societies have navigated this complex emotion over time.

Medium of Vent in Modern Societies

"A necessity for establishing emotional Equilibrium in the Society"

Contrary to the Traditional Societies, wherein the interdependence was limited and sufficient and institutionalized medium of vents existed , the modern society has shrinking anger spaces or medium of vents, which has resulted in an emotional disequilibrium and may be a potential cause for increase in crime rates as resort is being taken to the least scrutinized space of the cyber world.

In today's information societies, individuals continually encounter surveillance and maintain global interconnectedness, fostering a profound sense of interdependence. This interconnectedness, as emphasized by Durkheim in his theory, is a result of the specialized division of labor in modern society. This awareness of global interdependence may, however, restrict the space for individuals to openly express their anger. Even influential individuals may face challenges in expressing their anger openly due to the pervasive presence of mass surveillance and media scrutiny. In democratic societies, genuine power is derived from the masses, and this reality further complicates the open expression of anger for individuals in positions of authority.

The Compelling Need to Expand the Shrinking Anger Spaces for the "Greater Good"

The contemporary challenge at hand involves the intricate task of justifying traditional methods of anger management, especially considering the advocacy by animal rights activists for humane treatment. This heightened awareness underscores the imperative need for establishing spaces that not only acknowledge but also facilitate the constructive expression of anger by individuals. The absence of such outlets has the potential to contribute to mental health issues at the individual level, potentially giving rise to heightened anxiety.

Expanding this concern to a group level, the scarcity of channels for the expression of anger may contribute to an increase in instances of criminal behavior. The lack of constructive avenues for collective anger expression within societal frameworks could exacerbate social tensions, potentially resulting in an upswing in criminal activities.

On a broader community scale, unaddressed anger has the potential to escalate into more severe and complex issues, with terrorism being an extreme manifestation. Acknowledging and addressing the paramount importance of establishing healthy outlets for anger becomes crucial in navigating and mitigating these potential societal repercussions. Developing a comprehensive approach that considers the individual, group, and community levels is essential in fostering a balanced and emotionally healthy society.

While civilized means of expressing anger, such as engaging in debates, participating in sports competitions, and fostering discourses, and manage space for the peaceful protest, freedom of media. Many developing countries might not actively encourage these modern cultural practices rationally. It becomes imperative for societies to actively promote and increase spaces that facilitate the civilized expression of anger. The absence of such spaces can have detrimental effects on mental health, underscoring the importance of encouraging constructive and culturally relevant ways for individuals to articulate and manage their anger. Initiatives aimed at cultivating these spaces can contribute significantly to the overall well-being of individuals within a society.

"All that has come into being has to see its journey through, the advocacy for suppression of anger and anger-management techniques strive to achieve the impossible as an energy can neither be created nor be destroyed (like anger is an energy that cannot be destroyed) by can only be converted and channelized, the better the channelization, the effective the Society".

It is high time we gain a new perspective and count within the sources of energy not only -solar energy, wind energy, Hydro energy, and Geothermal energy but also – "Human Energy" which would include all emotions – "E-motion, Energy in Motion" namely and most significantly – "The Anger energy".

References:

Singh, S. (2021). The Psychology of Fashion: How Clothing Affects Our Mood and Behavior. Retrieved
from https://www.linkedin.com/pulse/psychology-fashion-how-clothing-affects-our-mood-behavior-singh-ex1mf

Wikipedia. (2023). Fashion. Retrieved
from https://en.wikipedia.org/wiki/Fashion

23

Chapter IV
The Risk of Emerging Virtual Inequality and Marginalization

Dr. Ashwani Kumar and Dr. Bachitter Singh

Society is understood as a complex network of human relationships, inherently unequal, leading to varying outcomes for different groups. These inequalities manifest as social exclusion, a dynamic process influenced by societal and historical contexts. For instance , the caste system in traditional Hindu society systematically excludes lower castes, embedding intergenerational inequities and hindering social mobility. State-centric or socialist societies exhibit exclusion through limited access to governmental roles, with marginalized individuals lacking authority and resources. In modern market-driven societies or capitalist societies, marginalization or exclusion is often linked to poverty, with neoliberalism and globalization intensifying economic divides and restricting access to resources and opportunities for the underprivileged. This economic marginalization reinforces poverty cycles and deepens social disparities.

The advent of the information age, especially the spread of the internet among masses has introduced new dynamics to society, i.e., the virtual society. Although the virtual society is an extension of mainstream society, at the same time it depicts a separate realm. Within the virtual society, similar to mainstream society, there is the presence of social differentiation. The dominant basis of this virtual social differentiation is the difference in the statuses roles of individuals (actors) in the virtual world. Generally, we can divide virtual actors' roles into influencers and followers. The influencers are those individuals who have a huge fan following or subscribers base; they can also be termed as virtual celebrities. While the followers are just the common internet users who follow the virtual celebrities; they can also be known as the virtual commoners.

The simple virtual role differentiation can gradually transform into social stratification as witnessed with various other differentiations in the past. In Bourdieu's framework, virtual influencers possess social capital in the form of followers. Those who lack virtual social capital or have a passive presence in the virtual platforms may be treated unequally. Similarly, it is also possible that those who have no presence in virtual platforms might be treated as uncivilized and could face discrimination in the virtual realm. This virtual inequality and discrimination could eventually lead to the marginalization of individuals and communities.

The individuals or actors who succeed in cultivating online influence may reinforce their dominance, further marginalizing the passive users. Bourdieu argued that in a social field individuals struggle or compete for various forms of capital. In the virtual social field, similar dynamics occur, where individuals compete for power and influence through their accumulation and deployment of *"Digital Capital"*. This digital capital can include factors such as technological proficiency, social media presence, access to information, and networking charisma and skills. Those who possess greater digital capital are better positioned to assert their dominance and dominate or marginalize others who lack these capabilities, perpetuating inequalities within the virtual realm.

The increased usage of the internet and social media or activity in virtual society, facilitated by advancements in information technology is redefining the dynamics of social interaction and power structures in contemporary society. Just as in conventional society, where individuals navigate social hierarchies based on factors such as wealth, status, and education, virtual society also witnesses the emergence of dominant figures (influencers) who wield influence and shape discourse on digital platforms.

As Michel Foucault suggests, knowledge is always generated by discourse, and eventually, that knowledge turns into power. In the context of virtual society, there are chances that those who hold dominant positions on digital platforms might develop the ability to shape and control discourse. Therefore, changes in discourse and the dissemination of knowledge can occur based on the interests and agendas of those in power within the virtual realm. This means that individuals or groups who dominate digital platforms can influence what information is circulated, how it is framed, and which perspectives are privileged or marginalized. Consequently, this control over discourse can further reinforce existing power structures or create new ones within the virtual space.

The distinctiveness of a virtual society stems from its reliance on virtual interaction platforms, commonly recognized as social media platforms like Facebook, Instagram, YouTube, and others. Each virtual platform is owned by individuals through companies, underscoring the significance of acknowledging that the popularity of the virtual society ultimately translates to the consolidation of societal ownership among a select group of businessmen. This scenario poses the risk of the prevailing democratic power structure evolving into an oligarchy or even a totalitarian system.

Actors in a virtual society engage in symbolic interactions through online communication, content creation, and digital presence. Their digital prowess allows them to shape narratives, set agendas, and influence public opinion, mirroring the dynamics of power and influence observed in conventional society. So, those individuals or communities who are already marginalized in mainstream society would further face marginalization in the virtual realm too, resulting in their double marginalization. Additionally, there are also risks of the rise of anti-social, anti-intellectual, deviant individuals or groups to get influence (in terms of followers) in the virtual platforms. They could not only further the marginalization but may also pose a threat to mainstream society by propagating anti-societal values, propaganda, extremism, and deviance. The dominance of such actors and marginalization of the genuine norm-abiding actors would be disrupting for the society as a whole.

The crucial question that arises is, are there any agencies or groups, either state or non-state, actively acknowledging this virtual phenomenon and formulating plans for affirmative actions to restrict or control virtual inequality and marginalization? Such initiatives or affirmative actions would not only provide an equitable platform for all individuals to express their opinions fairly but also prevent the emergence of new kinds of social inequalities and discrimination.

In the context of India, as with the majority of the world, individuals and market forces are increasingly switching to virtual interactions. In such a scenario, there is an urgent need to create an equitable virtual realm. While advancements in technology offer immense opportunities for connectivity and expression, the absence of sociological insights (or a contemporary socializing force to tackle the virtual realm) in the promotion of virtual platforms could result in furthering inequality. This opens up a problem similar to that highlighted by Weber in the *'fact-value distinction.'* For Weber, although science has made great advancements in various fields, especially technological one, it lacks or remains silent on the question of value, i.e., whether something is worth pursuing or not. There should always be a balance between facts and values, which can only be incorporated through sociological insights. By neglecting sociological considerations, we risk overlooking the opportunities that virtual spaces present, ultimately hindering inclusive societal progress. It would also result in various problems, such as inequality and marginalization, as highlighted in this article. Therefore, it is imperative for any society undergoing rapid digital transformation to incorporate sociological insights into policymaking and regulation of virtual spaces. Doing so will not only promote social cohesion and inclusivity but also mitigate the potential risks associated with unchecked digital expansion.

References:

1. Foucault, M. (1977). Discipline and punish: The birth of the prison. Vintage Books.

2. Weber, M. (1922). Economy and Society: An Outline of Interpretive Sociology (G. Roth & C. Wittich, Eds.). University of California Press.

3. Bourdieu, P. (1984). Distinction: A social critique of the judgment of taste. Harvard University Press.

4. Durkheim, E. (1895). The rules of sociological method. Free Press.

5. Castells, M. (1996). The rise of the network society (2nd ed.). Blackwell Publishers.

Chapter V

Exploring the Dynamics of Friendship

Dr. Ashwani Kumar

'It is the Simplest of concepts that require the Complex of Comprehension."

The Concept of Friendship is no exception to the afore-stated quote as all of us intuitively know – what friendship is, yet not all of us are successful in forging such relations and maintaining them.

In the common parlance, *"Any amicable interaction is qualified and understood as an interaction of friendship".* The Irony is the word "Amicable" is itself equated to the word "Friendly" and it is precisely the cause for the utter prevailing failures of the – "Institution of Friendship". As one mistakes every and each amicable (Hostile-free) interaction as an interaction of friendship and hastens to confer the status of "Friend" upon the interactor and self – confers upon oneself the same status, the problems arise and go to become the cause of the abysmal failure of the institution of friends.

It is crucial at this juncture to juxtapose the "Institution of friendship" as against the "Institution of Kinship" and institutionalize the Friendship interactions on the same lines of the "Institution of Kinship".

The Institution of Kinship: – "The First System of Institutionalized interactions".

In the history of social relations among individuals, every relationship is guided by social institutions. As we know, the foundation of traditional societies was kinship social organizations, and kinship relations in every society are guided by social institutions such as family, religion, and law. In every relationship, people interact with relatives, as status and roles of each status are defined by various social institutions. This enables even larger masses to fulfill the expectations of their relatives as defined by their status.

Kinship has long served as the cornerstone, providing a sense of predictability and certainty through fixed roles and expectations and the success of the same was rooted on the – "Institutionalization of the Interactions". It simpliciter implies the – "Prescription of – "How to carry out any interactions" and "Who would be the carriers of such interaction" and "What would be the interaction carried out".

The Prescriptions under 'How' refers to the – "Non-verbal aspect of the interaction including and not limited to demeanor, mannerisms and Etiquettes".

The Prescriptions under 'Who' refers to the – 'Status accorded on the "Interactor' and 'the Interacted' (in short status conferred on the interactors) example – "Status of the Interactor (Mother) and the Status of the Interacted (Son).

The Prescriptions under 'What' refers to the – 'Role and actions to be carried out played by the interactors". It is both Positive and Negative (i.e., What actions may be done and What should never be done).

Yet, in the mosaic of modern society, the landscape has evolved beyond the confines of familial ties. While professional relationships offer structure within defined roles, the emergence of friendship as a dominant relationship presents a nuanced challenge: the absence of clearly delineated roles within the status of a friend.

Institutionalization of the Interaction of Friendship – "A NEED"

Traditionally, kinship relations provided a framework within which individuals navigated their social world. Each kin status came with predetermined roles and expectations, promoting predictability and stability in interpersonal dynamics. However, as contemporary life unfolds, the centrality of kinship diminishes, and individuals find themselves drawn into the orbit of friendship.

Friendship, when viewed through a sociological lens, embodies a voluntary bond among individuals, transcending barriers of gender and age, rooted in reciprocity. This notion aligns with Aristotle's philosophical perspective, which categorizes friendships into three types: those of utility, pleasure, and virtue. Friendships of utility form around practical advantages, such as shared resources or skills, while friendships of pleasure emerge from mutual enjoyment of activities or interests. However, friendships of virtue, the highest form according to Aristotle, are grounded in admiration for each other's character and a shared commitment to moral excellence. These friendships foster mutual care and support, promoting personal growth and fulfillment. Integrating Aristotle's ideas, we understand that irrespective of societal conventions, friendships thrive on mutual benefit, shared experiences, and a genuine regard for each other's well-being.

Unlike kinship and other professional relations, the institution of friendship lacks the rigidity of defined roles. Instead, it thrives on fluidity, adaptability, and reciprocity. Like all other social relations, friendship also exhibits a variety. However, unlike other social relationships, friendship is an individualistic decision, signifying that individuals have to make a choice. This is acceptable for individuals who are enlightened and educated. However, nowadays, friendship is becoming decentralized, posing a risk. People might engage in friendship relations without being aware of their roles as friends. These types of individuals always rely on social institutions in the case of other relations, but in the case of friendship, there is no established social institution to guide the behaviour of friends. While this flexibility allows for organic growth and authenticity in relationships, it also introduces an element of uncertainty. In the absence of fixed roles, masses may struggle to discern their place within the dynamics of friendship, leading to ambiguity and confusion.

The contemporary landscape presents a paradox: while the need for personal connections remains as vital as ever, the structures that once provided stability—such as kinship—have eroded, leaving friendship as a dominant force. In navigating this terrain, individuals grapple with the tension between the desire for intimacy and the need for clarity in roles and expectations.

Consider a scenario where traditional kinship ties have weakened, and individuals turn to friendships for companionship, support, and belonging. In this context, the emergence of the status of a friend becomes paramount, yet the roles associated with this status remain nebulous. Friends may blur the lines between confidants, advisors, and companions, leading to ambiguity in expectations and interactions.

This ambiguity can manifest in various ways, from the struggle to define boundaries and responsibilities to the challenge of negotiating conflicts and navigating transitions. Without the guiding framework of fixed roles, individuals may find themselves adrift in a sea of uncertainty, unsure of where they stand or how to navigate the complexities of friendship.

However, within this uncertainty lies opportunity. The fluidity of friendship allows for unprecedented depth and richness in relationships, unbound by the constraints of tradition or expectation. As individuals embrace the complexity of friendship, they may discover new avenues for growth, connection, and self-discovery.

The emergence of friendship as a dominant relationship in contemporary society presents a unique challenge: the absence of clearly defined roles within the status of a friend. Yet, within this challenge lies the potential for profound connection and intimacy. Like all other social relations, friendship also exhibits a variety. However, unlike other social relationships, friendship is an individualistic decision, signifying that individuals have to make a choice. This is acceptable for individuals who are enlightened and educated. However, nowadays, friendship is becoming decentralized, posing a risk. People might engage in friendship relations without being aware of their roles as friends. These types of individuals always rely on social institutions in the case of other relationships, but in the case of friendship, there is no established social institution to guide the behavior of friends, as such the need to institutionalize the interaction of friendship is the need of the hour.

Based on the above discussion, we can infer that friendship might not be feasible for the masses. This is evident in the majority of people attempting to transform this relationship into various forms of relationships guided by established social institutions, such as pleasure partners, academic partners, professional partners, and so on. This suggests that for the masses, friendship serves as a means to establish other socially recognized relationships. Those who are unable to do so may struggle to form genuine friendships.

References:

1. Aristotle. (1999). Nicomachean ethics* (T. Irwin, Trans.). Hackett Publishing Company.

2. Bourdieu, P. (1984). Distinction: A social critique of the judgment of taste. Harvard University Press.

3. Foucault, M. (1977). Discipline and punish: The birth of the prison*. Vintage Books.

4. Weber, M. (1922). Economy and society: An outline of interpretive sociology (G. Roth & C. Wittich, Eds.). University of California Press.

5. Castells, M. (1996). The rise of the network society* (2nd ed.). Blackwell Publishers.

Chapter VI

Is Indian Society Experiencing Marketization in the Name of Modernization?

Dr. Ashwani Kumar and Dr. Bachitter Singh

"Modernism is about trusting in oneself, while marketism is about placing trust in the market."

Modernization is portrayed as the dominant force of Social Change

Modernization represents a transformative force that is reshaping societies globally. It embodies the unyielding quest for advancement, innovation, and the adaptation to emergent imperatives. This dynamic phenomenon enables nations, communities, and individuals to traverse the complexities of the contemporary era, adopting technological progress, socio-economic transformations, and cultural metamorphosis. In a world characterized by swift transitions, modernization acts as a catalyst for growth, development, and the aspiration towards an enhanced future. By incorporating digital technologies and advocating for sustainable methodologies, modernization alters every aspect of human life, presenting a spectrum of opportunities and challenges as societies endeavor to prosper in the twenty-first century

Classical sociologists such as Emile Durkheim, Max Weber, and Karl Marx offered diverse perspectives on modernity and modernization. Durkheim highlighted the transition from mechanical solidarity to organic solidarity as societies modernize. He emphasized the importance of social cohesion and the role of institutions in maintaining order amidst increasing complexity. On the other hand, Max Weber explored the rationalization and bureaucratization of modern societies. Weber's concept of the "iron cage" described the dehumanizing effects of rationalization, suggesting that modernization could lead to a loss of individual freedom and creativity. Karl Marx viewed modernization through the lens of class struggle and economic transformation. In "The Communist Manifesto," Marx critiqued capitalism as a driving force behind modernization, arguing that it perpetuated inequality and alienation. Despite their differing views, these classical sociologists collectively underscored the profound societal changes accompanying modernization, while struggling with its implications for social order, individual autonomy, and economic structure.

Giddens views modernity as a reflexive process driven by globalization, technology, and the interplay between structure and agency, encapsulating the emergence of a risky society characterized by unprecedented societal transformations and the need for constant adaptation.

Modernity Misinterpreted in India

In his work "Mistaken Modernity," Dipankar Gupta offers a new perspective on the concept of modernity, challenging the common notion prevalent in India that equates it solely with technological advancement or increased consumption. Instead, Gupta underscores that modernity encompasses far more than material progress; it is intertwined with the attitudes and social dynamics shaping a society. Central to Gupta's critique is the Indian middle class, which he observes to superficially adopt aspects of modernity while concurrently holding onto traditional values. This dichotomy is particularly evident in various aspects of societal life, including familial relationships, the persistence of caste and social hierarchies, and a selective adherence to legal norms. Gupta coins the term *"west-toxicated class"* to encapsulate this phenomenon, highlighting how Western ideals influence certain segments of society without fully embracing the transformative aspects of modernity. Through his analysis, Gupta prompts a critical reflection on the complexities of modernization in Indian society, urging for a more holistic understanding that transcends superficial appearances.

"Marketization Taking Precedence Over Modernization in Indian Society"

In the Indian context, modernisation and urbanisation are often conflated with the expansion of market cities. However, it's crucial to recognize that while modernization involves adopting new technologies and social structures, urbanization specifically pertains to the growth of urban areas and the migration of people from rural to urban settings.

We observe in India not merely modernization but a significant shift towards marketization.

Marketization refers to the increasing influence of market forces on various aspects of society, including economic, social, and cultural domains. In the Indian context, this phenomenon is evident in the rapid growth of urban centers driven by market demands. As technology and production systems modernize, they integrate more deeply with market mechanisms, shaping societal structures and norms.

The decision-making process of individuals, both with and without assets in rural areas, reflects this marketization trend. Those with assets may choose to remain in rural areas, but their lifestyles and consumption patterns often align with market-driven aspirations. Conversely, those without assets seek better opportunities in urban areas, where the allure of market-driven livelihoods and amenities is strong.

As individuals transition from rural to urban settings, they become integral parts of the market ecosystem as consumers or producers. This integration reinforces the dominance of market forces in shaping societal dynamics. The emergence of a *"market-toxicated"* class, primarily in urban areas, underscores the pervasive influence of market ideologies on individual aspirations and lifestyles. A significant portion of the urban population becomes part of what can be termed a "market-toxicated" class, meaning they imagine their lives solely within the confines of market spaces.

This market-toxicated class diversifies the market, creating different market spaces for different socioeconomic classes. The elite class, represented by the business class, emerges as the primary beneficiaries of this market system. The middle class, which manages to secure a place in the market, remains dependent on it, thus comprising a substantial portion of the market-toxicated masses.

Even among the lower classes in contemporary Indian society, there exists a subset who, despite their limited resources, choose to adapt to the norms and values of the market-based society. These individuals manage to sustain themselves with a low quality of life, often scraping by with minimal financial means. However, alongside this group exists a significant portion of the population known as the *'pennyless class'*. These individuals lack the resources necessary for survival in the competitive landscape of market-driven spaces.

In contemporary times, especially, the prevalence of this pennyless class is notable. They are the ones who have failed to secure even the basic financial resources needed for sustenance. Unfortunately, in the current Indian societal framework, there is a dearth of inclusive policies tailored to support individuals in such precarious financial situations.

As a result of their dire economic circumstances, the cognition and regulation of the penniless class are profoundly constrained. Their everyday lives are overshadowed by the constant struggle for survival in a society dominated by market dynamics. This struggle often develops a sense of *'marketxiety'* among the economically marginalized class. 'Marketxiety' is the stress and fear experienced by individuals associated with how they regulate their lives in the market.

The likelihood of marketxiety being more prevalent among the penniless class has the potential to escalate into what can be termed as *"politicsxiety"*—a deep-seated mistrust or fear towards the prevailing political system. Dipanker Gupta's exploration sheds light on how urbanization and masculinity intertwine to promote what he terms "manxiety," primarily affecting men who become victims of masculinity in the urban centers, but there are chances marketxiety affects both genders.

As these anxieties intensify, individuals may feel increasingly marginalized and disenfranchised within society. This sense of alienation can drive them towards resorting to unlawful activities as a means of survival. However, each unlawful act further exacerbates their fear of being disconnected from mainstream society.

In a market-based society, where the penniless class is already on the fringes of mainstream social structures, the temptation to engage in unlawful activities as a means of survival becomes even more pronounced. The lack of viable alternatives and the constant struggle for basic necessities can push individuals towards desperate measures, perpetuating a vicious cycle of marginalization and criminality.

The introduction of modern forces in India has been profoundly shaped by market influences, leading to a widespread misconception of modernity as synonymous with consumption. This misinterpretation has fueled the rapid expansion of marketization across various sectors of Indian society. Consequently, the pursuit of modernization has become entangled with the proliferation of market forces, resulting in a landscape where economic imperatives often overshadow broader societal goals.

Furthermore, in Indian society, people are experiencing marketization in the name of modernization. Notably, the Indian market not only promotes modern scientific values and materials but also actively promotes traditional values. This dual promotion creates a complex cultural landscape where traditional and modern values intertwine within the framework of market dynamics.

References:

1. Gupta, D. (2000). Mistaken modernity: India between worlds*. Harper Collins Publishers India.
2. Sen, A. (2000). Development as freedom. Oxford University Press.

3. Appadurai, A. (1996). Modernity at large: Cultural dimensions of globalization*. University of Minnesota Press.

4. Chakrabarty, D. (2000). Provincializing Europe: Postcolonial thought and historical difference. Princeton University Press.

Chapter VII

Social Media Reels and Clothing Consumption: Exploring Trends, Influence, and Sustainability

Amit Kumar

Social media has revolutionized human connectivity and interaction, weaving a complex network that spans across global communities. Its diverse platforms, from Facebook to Instagram, Twitter, and others, have fostered a seamless exchange of thoughts, experiences, and emotions, transcending geographical confines (Tierney, T. 2013). These platform has emerged as a significant influencer, shaping cultural trends, amplifying diverse voices, and serving as a virtual hub where individuals craft identities, build connections, and navigate the dynamic digital landscape. Despite its far-reaching impact, concerns linger around privacy, mental well-being, and the spread of misinformation. However, amidst these complexities, social media continues to stand as an unparalleled facilitator of connectivity, fostering the exchange of ideas, celebrating diversity, and empowering voices that might otherwise remain marginalized or overlooked (Van Dijck, J. 2013).

Human society is fundamentally shaped by the nature of human interactions, changes in these interactions profoundly impact various aspects of human life.(Prus, R. 1995). The advancements in science and technology have not only made human connections more inclusive but also intricate and fraught with risks. As Anthony Giddens, a renowned sociologist, introduced the notion of the "risk society" in his influential writings. His argument centered on the evolution of modern societies, which progressively find themselves entangled in risks resulting from the very progress and innovations aimed at improving our existence. This shift relegates conventional risk sources like natural disasters and diseases to a secondary role, overshadowed by the risks born out of human actions, technological advancements, and scientific pursuits (Giddens, 1999). The advent of modern industrial practices has led to the emergence of unsustainable living patterns. Unsustainable living encompasses behaviors that significantly contribute to environmental degradation, depletion of vital resources, and overall harm to the planet. This lifestyle often involves excessive consumption, heavy reliance on non-renewable resources, wasteful practices, a disregard for environmental consequences, and a lack of consideration for the long-term impact of personal actions on the planet. Conversely, sustainable living represents a conscious lifestyle choice aimed at minimizing one's environmental footprint. It involves deliberate efforts to reduce waste, conserve resources, and promote long-term ecological balance. This lifestyle advocates for practices such as decreasing energy consumption, utilizing renewable resources, engaging in recycling and composting, supporting local and ethical products, and adopting eco-friendly habits to foster a more harmonious relationship with the environment.

From our preceding discussion, it's evident that the sustainability of life hinges on human consumption habits. Excessive consumption is inherently detrimental to the planet, amplifying the risks of unsustainability. This study specifically examines how the proliferation of social media reels influences the clothing consumption patterns among young individuals. Social media reels, comprising short, captivating video clips shared across various platforms, serve as a vehicle for individuals to express their choices, preferences, and hobbies. These platforms, from a sociological perspective, offer a means to showcase one's consumption patterns. Thorstein Veblen, a prominent sociologist from the late 19th century, introduced the concept of "conspicuous consumption" in his book "The Theory of the Leisure Class," published in 1899. Veblen coined this term to delineate the phenomenon where individuals exhibit their wealth and social status through extravagant and often unnecessary spending on goods and services. He highlighted how this behavior is driven by the pursuit of social recognition and the desire to signal one's elevated social standing within a community.

There have been numerous studies delving into how social media contributes to the proliferation of conspicuous consumption, establishing a positive correlation between conspicuous behavior and an increase in unsustainable living, impacting both humans and other species. Compulsive buying behavior, as identified by Faber and Christenson (1996), is associated with potential causes rooted in biochemical, psychological, or societal factors. This behavior manifests as uncontrolled and excessive purchasing, as noted by Billieux et al. (2008), often triggered by internal tensions or frustration, compelling individuals to engage in compulsive spending. The allure lies in the short-term gratification and transient relief these purchases offer, serving as a means to momentarily alter or elevate one's mood.

Moreover, conspicuous buying behavior, commonly observed among social media users, is characterized by individuals following consumption trends influenced by herd behavior, seeking validation from peers and influencers. Impulsive buyers frequently demonstrate conspicuous consumption tendencies by purchasing flashy products endorsed by influencers or deemed trendy within their social circles. In a study by Changchit et al. (2019), a notable surge in Thai social media usage was observed, rising from 18 to 32 hours per week between 2015 and 2018, concurrent with nearly doubling online expenditure during this period. Their survey outcomes, illustrating a 70% likelihood of social media users engaging with newsfeed advertisements, corroborate with Digital's (2021) insights. Specifically, Digital's data underscores Facebook (38%) and Instagram (37%) as platforms with the highest rates of ad click-throughs.

According to Digital 2023,In the early months of 2023, India demonstrated a robust digital landscape, marking significant milestones in internet connectivity, social media engagement, and mobile communication. The country began the year with an impressive count of 692.0 million internet users, illustrating a substantial 48.7 percent penetration rate. Alongside this, India accommodated a vast social media community, tallying 467.0 million users, which accounted for 32.8 percent of the nation's total population. Additionally, the proliferation of mobile connectivity reached remarkable heights, with India boasting an extensive 1.10 billion active cellular mobile connections, encompassing a striking 77.0 percent of the entire population. These statistics underscore India's active participation and engagement in the digital sphere, reflecting a growing reliance and integration of technology into the daily lives of its citizens.

This study probe deeply into how the prevalent trend of sharing reels among young individuals amplifies their inclination to purchase more clothing items. Clothing, beyond its utilitarian function of protecting the body, holds substantial symbolic value across cultures, often serving as a status symbol. In the study by Entwistle, J. (2023) Clothing and style aren't just about aesthetics; they're intertwined with societal constructs, influencing how we perceive and express identity, culture, and social dynamics. As noted by Zaheer Ahmad, et al. (2008) social media interactions transcend cultural barriers, fostering connections among diverse populations. Consequently, the exposure to different cultural clothing styles and trends on social media platforms augments the likelihood of increased clothing purchases. Since public nudity isn't socially acceptable in any culture, the manifestation of one's identity through reels underscores the intimate connection between an individual's identity and their choice of clothing. This link between self-expression and attire showcased on social media platforms further reinforces the significance of clothing in shaping and projecting one's identity within the digital realm.

Cláudio (2007) noted Clothing production spans a spectrum, utilizing both organic and synthetic materials. Organic materials, sourced from nature, encompass cotton, wool, silk, hemp, and bamboo. Grown or processed without synthetic chemicals, these materials boast biodegradability and a reputation for environmental friendliness.

Conversely, synthetic fabrics such as polyester, nylon, rayon, and spandex are human-engineered from chemical compounds. These fabrics often tout durability, moisture-wicking properties, and specialized functionalities. However, their non-biodegradable nature and the environmental toll incurred during their production process raise concerns.

Remarkably, the soaring demand for both organic and synthetic clothing poses challenges to sustainable living. The amplified desire for organic garments accelerates the extraction of natural resources, intensifying the risk of unsustainable practices. Conversely, the proliferation of synthetic materials amplifies pollution concerns due to their non-biodegradable nature and the environmental footprint associated with their production. Striking a balance between consumer demand, responsible sourcing, and environmentally conscious manufacturing processes remains pivotal in steering the fashion industry towards more sustainable practices and reducing its ecological impact.

References

1. Tierney, T. (2013). *The public space of social media: Connected cultures of the network society.* Routledge.

2. Van Dijck, J. (2013). *The culture of connectivity: A critical history of social media.* Oxford University Press.

3. Entwistle, J. (2023). *The fashioned body: Fashion, dress and modern social theory.* John Wiley & Sons.

4. Zaheer Ahmad, Saira Hanif Soroya & Khalid Mahmood. (2023) Bridging social capital through the use of social networking sites: A systematic literature review. *Journal of Human Behavior in the Social Environment* 33:4, pages 473-489.

5. Cláudio, L. (2007). Waste Couture: Environmental impact of the clothing industry. *Environmental Health Perspectives, 115*(9). https://doi.org/10.1289/ehp.115-a449

6. Prus, R. (1995). *Symbolic interaction and ethnographic research: Intersubjectivity and the study of human lived experience.* State University of New York Press.

About the Authors

1	Dr. Ashwani Kumar is an Assistant Professors in UILS (Sociology), Chandigarh University. He has completed his PhD from Panjab University, Chandigarh, India.

2	Dr. Bachitter Singh is working as a Faculty (Sociology) in Ramnagar Campus, University of Jammu, India. He has completed his PhD in Sociology from Panjab University, Chandigarh, India.

3	Dr. Vikas Bhandari is an Assistant Professors in UILS (Political Science), Chandigarh University

4	Mr. Arvind is a Law student at Chandigarh University, Punjab (India).

5	Mr. Amit Kumar is currently working as an Assistant Professor (Sociology) in Gurukashi University, Punjab, India.